DESTINATION: LIFE

NAVIGATING YOUR FUTURE WITH JESUS

············

40 DEVOTIONS

MIKAL KEEFER | STORM

JESUS-CENTERED DEVOTIONS J.

Jesus-Centered Devotions
Destination: Life
Navigating Your Future With Jesus

group.com
Authors: Mikal Keefer and Storm
Chief Creative Officer: Joani Schultz
Senior Editor: Candace McMahan
Art Director: Jeff Storm
Cover Art: Jeff Storm
Production Manager: Melissa Towers

ISBN: 978-1-4707-4844-9

10 9 8 7 6 5 4 3 2 1   26 25 24 23 22 21 20 19 18 17

Printed in China.

"What's next? I wish I knew…"

Graduation is one of those milestones that prompts everyone to ask: What's next? And then what's after that?

Like it's possible to lay out the next 20 stops in life. While still sipping punch at your graduation party.

When asked about your "end game" or "long-range plans," do this: Say you're waiting to see where Jesus leads. And that you'd appreciate any prayer along those lines.

Your answer will scare off half the people asking the question and intrigue the other half. And very likely surface a handful of Jesus-followers who lean in and say, "Me, too."

Those are people worth getting to know. And asking to pray for you.

Mission accomplished.

{ *Your mom always bought Cheerios—but you don't have to. Choose for yourself what you like, don't like, believe, and don't believe.* }

Draw a simple tree—one with a wide trunk and branches coming out of it. Ask Jesus for a word or a phrase that represents the "trunk" of your future—what sort of life he's calling you to.

Write what you hear on the trunk, and then ask Jesus to show you some of the ways you might be able to live out that calling. Write those on the branches.

THE JOURNEY

ISN'T ABOUT WHERE YOU GO.

IT'S ABOUT
WHO YOU'RE WITH.

Be All In

Not about everything in life, but about something.
About someone.

Jesus is an all-in, everything-or-nothing kind of guy. He's not interested in launching a fan club; he wants followers.

Maybe that's why he said this: "Whoever is not with me is against me, and whoever does not gather with me scatters" (Matthew 12:30).

Now that you're grown up...now that being a Jesus-follower isn't a matter of drifting along on family faith, habit, or tradition... now that following requires a decision...

What do you do with what Jesus said?

Work your butt off. That's how you earn the respect of professors and bosses.

Tell Jesus if you're in...out...or making up your mind about him right here. **Right now.**

JESUS, I AM...

all for your plans for me

What breaks your heart?

You can learn a lot about people by watching what breaks their hearts, what grabs their full attention and won't let go.

Jesus was often delayed by compassion. He's rushing along to the next town and encounters blind men (Matthew 20:34) or a leper (Mark 1:40-41). He sees a crowd of hungry people (Mark 8:2) and pauses to meet their needs.

The hurting. The needy. The grieving. The widowed, orphaned, and abandoned. Those were the people Jesus couldn't seem to pass by without letting them know: I see you. I love you.

As you come to know Jesus better, you'll find yourself caring more about what he cares about. *Who* he cares about. And you'll come to understand that being delayed by compassion? That's no delay at all—it's the most important opportunity of your day.

Who in your life would Jesus stop to touch? Who'd get a kind word from him?

{ *You should for sure care about others. However, in shared* }
{ *showers wear flip-flops for reasons too disgusting to mention.* }

Ask Jesus to guide you as you jot down some names. Then ask him to give you both the opportunity and nudge to reach out on his behalf.

This...is enough.

One fast way to become happier is to choose contentment. To decide that what you have in life is okay. To let it be enough for now.

Paul wrote this: "I know what it is to be in need, and I know what it is to have plenty. I have learned the secret of being content in any and every situation, whether well fed or hungry, whether living in plenty or in want. I can do all this through him who gives me strength" (Philippians 4:12-13).

It's one thing to write that sentiment while sitting in the closest Starbucks, latté in hand. It's another to write it where Paul found himself: Under arrest and possibly awaiting execution.

But Paul could be content because, regardless of his surroundings, he was with Jesus...and that was enough for him.

What about you? Is Jesus enough? You can't make him enough, but he can make *himself* enough. When we see what a treasure Jesus is, then having that treasure with us is enough.

{ *"My GPA won't matter in heaven. My GPA won't matter in heaven. My GPA won't matter in heaven."—Anonymous* }

If you were to decide to be content, what might need to shift in your attitude today? Jot down your thoughts.

THINGS YOU MIGHT NOT WANT TO BE CONTENT WITH...

{ } Living without that amazing curbside couch. Muscle it onto the roof of your car and loop ropes through open windows and around the couch. Tie securely—*after* you're in the car. Drive slowly.

{ } Stinky dirty clothes. Just remember the basic groupings and water temp formula: whites/lights, delicates, towels and jeans, and darks. Don't over-stuff the washer. Wash dark loads in cold and whites in warm. *(Take the extra step and make your mom proud. Try ironing your shirts.)*

{ } A toxic bathroom. Flu and all sorts of other bacteria love a dirty bathroom. Keep your toothbrush as far from the toilet as you can. Tests prove that toothbrushes even three feet away from the toilet can get backsplash on them.

{ } An idiot. Even if he's tan and attractive, don't date him.

{ } Soggy crust on left-over pizza. Just place a cup of water in the microwave with the pizza and—voilà! No soggy crust.

05

"And this is supposed to make me happy?"

Jesus had an unusual view of what it takes to be happy.

He said, "God blesses you when people mock you and persecute you and lie about you and say all sorts of evil things against you because you are my followers. Be happy about it! Be very glad! For a great reward awaits you in heaven" (Matthew 5:10-12, NLT).

Thumbs up for a reward in heaven, but in the meantime, that's a lot of harassment, insults, and snarky comments to navigate.

Let alone to be *happy* about navigating.

But maybe Jesus was saying that faithfulness leads to deep joy. And if you're suffering on his behalf—because you're living out your faith, not because you're obnoxiously pointing out the faults of others—that's a good thing.

It means you're walking with Jesus closely enough that people around you see and feel it. See and feel him. You're reflecting his values and concerns in a world that's never embraced those easily.

If that's the case—be happy. You're right where you need to be.

{ *Living in a dorm? Prop your door open often. Great way to spontaneously meet people and indicate you're up for new friendships.* }

In what ways do people around you know you're a Jesus-follower? Are you feeling accepted—maybe even celebrated—for who you are, or do you feel harassed and insulted for it? Find a way, right now, to thank Jesus for either response.

I feel accepted for who I am, and I'm going to thank Jesus by...

I feel harassed for who I am, and I'm going to thank Jesus by...

06

"So it's okay for Christians to be sad?"

Not just sad—*heartbroken*.

Who decided that, if you know Jesus, you've no justifiable reason to be sad? That sorrow means a lack of faith and hope?

Thank God that Jesus never got that memo.

As Jesus made his way into Jerusalem, cheered on by the crowd around him, he could see what was coming for the city: destruction—and soon. Some of the children laying palm leaves in his path would live to see Rome thunder in and crush Jerusalem.

And Jesus wept.

His sadness wasn't for himself, but for others. It was borne out of a deep empathy, a desire that all should know him and the joy of his peace.

Jesus wept for those whose lives were poorer because they wouldn't or couldn't embrace him. His heart still breaks for them.

{ *When nothing goes right, go left.* }

What's breaking your heart right now, and why?
What brings you to tears? Write or draw it here.

BROKENHEARTED BROKENHEARTED BROKENHEARTED BROKENHEARTED BROKENHEARTED BROKENHEARTED BROKENHEARTED BROKENHEARTED BROKENHEARTED BROKENHEARTED BROKENHEARTED BROKENHEARTED BROKENHEARTED BROKENHEARTED BROKENHEARTED BROKENHEARTED BROKENHEARTED BROKENHEARTED BROKENHEARTED BROKENHEARTEDBROK BROKENHEARTEDBROKENHEARTED BROKENHEARTED BROKENHEARTED BROKENHEARTED BROKENHEARTED BROKENHEARTED BROKENHEARTED BROKENHEARTED BROKENHEARTED BROKENHEARTED

Ramen Noodles make everything better.

Some Quick Ramen Recipes Anyone Can Make

RAMEN MARINARA

You need:
1 pkg any flavor ramen noodles
1/2 cup spaghetti sauce

What to do:
Cook noodles and drain. Heat sauce
and pour over noodles.

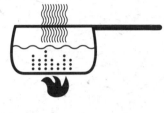

CHINESE STYLE RAMEN

You need:
1 pkg Asian ramen noodles
1 tsp soy sauce

What to do:
Cook noodles and drain. Add seasoning
packet. Add soy sauce to taste.

BEEFY RAMEN

You need:
1 pkg beef ramen noodles
1 tsp Worcestershire sauce

What to do:
Cook noodles and drain.
Add seasoning packet. Add
Worcestershire sauce to taste.

07

"I miss my old life."

It's okay if you're homesick.

If not for home, exactly, then for those days when someone else was responsible for keeping you warm, fed, and safe. When your happiness mattered so much to others that you could take their love for granted.

Who wouldn't miss that?

Well, those days aren't gone. The people who loved you then love you now. And the truth is that the one you probably took most for granted isn't living back in the old neighborhood. He's with you now.

Jesus said even the hairs of your head are all numbered (Mathew 10:30), so you can be assured he's up on what's happening in the wonderful world of you.

Jesus knows you, loves you, walks with you.

And anywhere Jesus is? That's home.

Songs attach themselves to memories, so make a playlist of songs that remind you of the good things from your past.

Today, call or text a few of the people you miss. Remind them you love them—and tell them why. Ask Jesus to put a few names on your heart; then list who you'll call or text below:

THINGS WE STILL ASK MOM

How do I make a dentist appointment?
How do I thaw a chicken?
Can I have your Netflix login?
How many stamps do I put on something?
Is it Dad's birthday?
How do you cook rice?
How do I get credit?
How do I un-sign up for a credit card?
Do I need a tetanus shot?
How do I wash something?
Do I have any allergies I don't know about?

08

Who *is* this guy?

"When the Temple guards returned without having arrested Jesus, the leading priests and Pharisees demanded, 'Why didn't you bring him in?'

"'We have never heard anyone speak like this!' the guards responded" (John 7:45-46, NLT).

That's right: The very guys sent to arrest Jesus were so stunned by how he spoke that they couldn't bring themselves to do their jobs.

Most rabbis talked *about* God the same way they talked about Moses—they knew a lot about him, but it wasn't like they were on a first-name basis. They'd never actually *met* the guy.

But Jesus? He was different. He knew God...talked with God... talked *as* God.

He talked like nobody before...or since. And he's talking still.

The question is: What's he saying to you?

{Tough Choices #3: Do I study more, or do I take the Buzzfeed quiz to see what kind of Poptart I am?}

START DOODLING.

Then ask Jesus to actually direct your doodles. Maybe Jesus has something to say to you through them, so doodle as a child would, and let Jesus surface something in you. Accept what comes, and pay attention to it. Ask Jesus what he's wanting to communicate to you.

09

You can count on me.

"For where your treasure is, there your heart will be also" (Matthew 6:21).

Jesus said that—and he wasn't really talking about money. He was talking about what we value most in life. He knows our hearts follow what we value most.

There's a *lot* of competition for your heart. Your job or studies, friendships, family, your bank balance—they all elbow one another for your heart. And whatever you give your attention to—especially your best attention—that's where your heart follows.

So, two questions for you: What does your heart value most? Where is your treasure buried?

{ *Never give up. Great things take time.* }

Draw your answer to those questions here. Where's your heart invested?

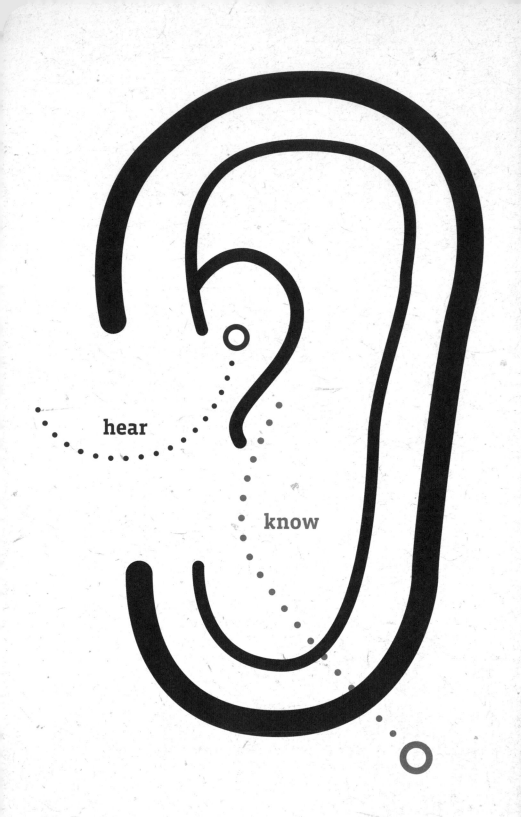

hear

know

Jesus who?

It's easy to feel indignant when you're ignored.

When your older co-workers hear your idea, push it aside, then think they've reinvented gravity when they stumble across the same idea later.

It's annoying when others don't value what you bring to the table.

For a guy who could raise the dead and pull thousands of fish sandwiches out of a basket, Jesus got ignored—a *lot*.

People heard what he said—and promptly forgot about it. Which wasn't—and still isn't—smart. Or healthy.

Jesus told a story about two people who built houses, one on the beach and one on a rock. You can read it in Matthew 7:24-27, but here's a quick summary: Knowing what Jesus said is nice, but it won't give you a firm foundation. Standing strong during storms happens when you know Jesus well enough to do what he says to do.

{ *College student physics: A student in bed will remain* }
{ *in bed unless acted upon by a large enough panic.* }

Draw your dream house. On the foundation write a few words that describe Jesus' "rock" attributes. What exactly makes him a firm foundation?

And, yes, this is a metaphor...

"I could use a break."

"Come to me, all you who are weary and burdened, and I will give you rest. Take my yoke upon you and learn from me, for I am gentle and humble in heart, and you will find rest for your souls."

—Jesus (Matthew 11:28-29)

Come to *me*.

I will give you rest.

Take *my* yoke.

Learn from *me*.

Notice: It's all about Jesus. He's at the exact center of where you'll find real rest and refreshment. He's your soul oasis.

People listening to Jesus that day knew all about yokes—hardware slipped over the necks and shoulders of animals expected to trudge through their day pulling heavy burdens. Those listening to Jesus had long believed they had to earn God's favor by obeying rules—rules they couldn't possibly keep.

Now it was all about Jesus. About forgiveness. About grace.

It's *still* all about Jesus.

{ *Haunted house idea: People pop out and ask you what you're doing after graduation.* }

In what ways—if any—are you burdened? While having a conversation with Jesus about how he wants you to come to him...rest in him...learn from him, start scribbling out the burdens in words or images.

REST

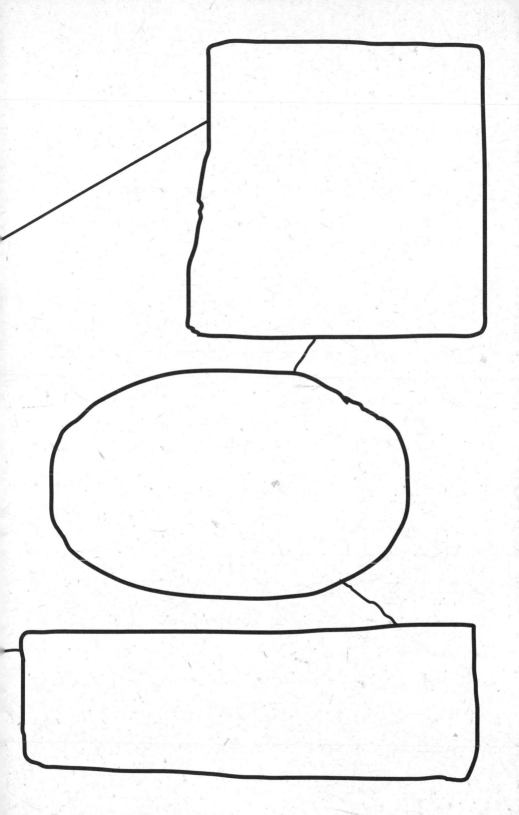

"If I can do only one thing today…"

Jesus was pretty clear about his priorities for you: Love God with all that's in you, and love others the way you'd like to be loved.

Love. That pretty much covers it.

If you're wondering how that looks when lived out, slow down and pay ridiculous attention to Jesus.

He said he did only those things his Father directed him to do. He made time to connect with God. And he focused intently on the needs of people around him.

You're not Jesus, but you have his Spirit living in you. And you're likely the only Jesus some people in your life will meet today.

Feel free to tackle all the projects on your plate. But be open to a gentle nudging to pause and connect with a friend, co-worker, or someone you've just met…to trade in urgent stuff for important stuff. To come up for air and notice—really notice—people in your life.

Love them the way you'd like to be loved. The way Jesus loves you.

And thank Jesus for how he's loving you.

Friend text: Feel like a run? Me text: You spelled "wanna get tacos" wrong.

Who are you being nudged to connect with?

How are you going to notice them?

Adulting sometimes feels a little like those times when you used to play Mario Kart and you thought you were in first place, then you realized you were looking at the wrong screen and crashing into walls.

13

Welcome to Roommate World

(Where Patience Goes to Die)

When you pictured yourself out on your own, you probably didn't factor in a roommate who snores. Has never once taken out the trash. "Borrows" liberally from your closet. Invites overnight guests who then all but move in.

Yeah...that wasn't part of the deal. Until it was.

How to cope?

Some clear boundaries and direct communication will help. And there's this:

"Then Peter came to Jesus and asked, 'Lord, how many times shall I forgive my brother or sister who sins against me? Up to seven times?'

"Jesus answered, 'I tell you, not seven times, but seventy-seven times" (Matthew 18:21-22).

So, does this mean Jesus would let a thoughtless roommate do whatever he or she wanted, with no consequences? Or might Jesus find a way to both forgive and expose his roommate's poor behavior and invite repentance?

Whatever your tough situation, stop to ask Jesus what he would have you do.

(Get the whole story by reading Matthew 18:21-35.)

{ *Roomate Note #1: Dear Cody, my parents are coming for a visit today. Can you please wear pants all day?* }

Draw a picture of what you sense Jesus is asking you
to do about your tough situation.

THEN SCRIBBLE WILDLY OVER THE PAGE WITH
RECKLESS ABANDON. IT HAS A CALMING EFFECT.

ROOMATE CONTRACT

THOU SHALT NOT LEAVE THE
OVEN ON...AND KILL US ALL.

IF YOU SEE THE SPIDER, YOU
KILL THE SPIDER.

WEAR YOUR OWN CLOTHES.

PUT SOME CLOTHES ON.

STOP HITTING THE SNOOZE
BUTTON.

REALIZE YOU'RE NOT ALWAYS
RIGHT.

THIS IS A LEGALLY BINDING DOCUMENT.

I AM THE GOOD SHEPHERD.

I KNOW MY SHEEP AND THEY KNOW ME.

THEY LISTEN TO MY VOICE.

—JESUS

14

"Why don't they just mind their own business?"

Plenty of people have plans for your future now that you've graduated.

Your career...love life...next academic steps.

So who gets a vote? Whose advice counts? Everyone's? No one's?

Jesus said those who follow him hear his voice—and listen. So in the howl of opinions, the avalanche of well-intentioned advice, tune into the two voices that matter most.

His. And yours.

In that order.

{ Awkward Moment #5: Not sure if you have actual free time, or you're just forgetting everything. }

Jot down what you're hearing from Jesus...and yourself:

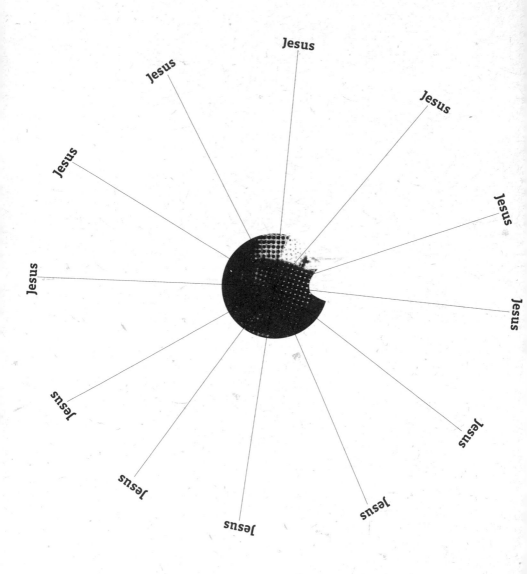

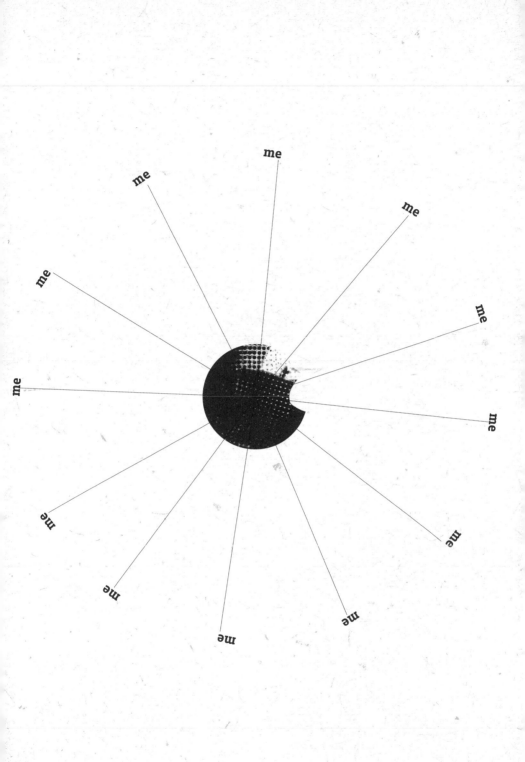

15

What the...?

If you sometimes get angry, you're not alone. Jesus also got fired up. As in whip-wielding, flip-over-tables fired up. And in the Temple courtyard, no less.

Of course, it was *his* Temple, and people he sent scattering were defiling it. Freaking out because someone cut you off in traffic doesn't really compare.

But think about it: Angry Jesus. Furious Jesus. Kicking-butt-and-taking-names Jesus, not one inch of "meek and mild" peeking out around the edges.

What do you do with that Jesus? Jesus who chooses to not let an injustice stand? who determines the most loving thing to do is to call people on Their Stuff? Do you like him...or not?

(See John 2:13-22 for a description of Supremely Annoyed Jesus.)

The more underwear you have, the less you have to do laundry.

In what ways—if any—does picturing Angry Jesus color your feelings about him?

Thoughts?

16

"I'm just keeping it real."

Authenticity = good stuff.

Jesus is all for authenticity. He often helped people see themselves for who they really were.

One guy was rich—but his money strangled his spiritual health. Another looked holy but was a hypocrite. And yes, people hated Zacchaeus, but they didn't see what Jesus saw: someone desperate for a new life, desperate for rescue from shame and self-hatred.

That's the thing about Jesus-style authenticity: He doesn't see only who you are, but who you were *created* to be. And if there's a gap, he'll walk across it with you.

So who are you—authentically? Who Did Jesus create you to be?

(Check out those authenticity encounters: Mark 10:17-27; Matthew 23:27-28; and Luke 19:1-10.)

{ *Stretch. You're officially getting older—stay limber by stretching.* }

What words describe who you are...and who you were created to be? If there's a gap, ask Jesus how he might narrow it with you.

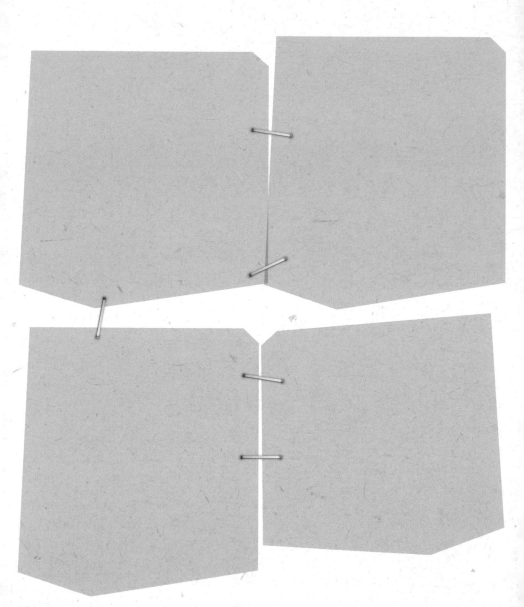

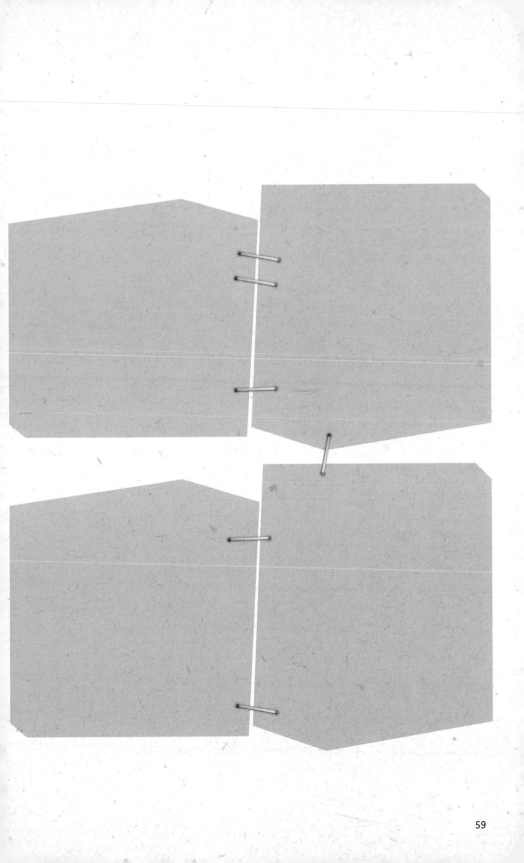

17

"I'm bored."

We can fix that for you. Pick one:

Write a thank you note to someone who's been kind to you.
Call a parent. Pray with someone. Pray *for* someone. Clean
out your closet; then donate quality used stuff. Volunteer. Ask
an elderly person for a story from his or her life. Compliment
someone—and be specific. Walk around picking up trash for five
minutes. Wave to a neighbor. Post a positive review. Applaud a
kid. Sit with a hospital patient. Organize a fundraiser or launch
a Kickstarter for a worthy cause. Notice something amazing in
nature and congratulate God on a job well done. Go do good. Go
be good. When you do, you're not only acting like Jesus; you're
worshipping him with your life.

When you've got *those* wrapped up, circle back. There's always
more.

Better yet, boredom-proof your own life.

{ *Fact: The average person visits the toilet 2,500 times a year. That's six to
eight times a day. Which means, on average, you can expect to spend
three years on the toilet. Your're there right now, aren't you?* }

Put a pen in your mouth; then use it
to draw a path through the maze.

start

boredom busted

And my God will meet all your needs according to the riches of his glory in Christ Jesus.

Philippians 4:19

18

"Maybe they're right...I *am* a loser."

Not so fast. You're more than your most recent screw-up. Much more.

If you could see yourself as Jesus sees you, you'd know. Know why he willingly shouldered your cross, why he reaches out to you with infinite love, enduring patience, and fierce devotion. Yes, you're a sheep—metaphorically speaking—and if you've spent much time around sheep, you know that's not really a good thing. But you have a Good Shepherd who loves you.

You are loved. By Jesus. Right now.

If you saw yourself fresh, through Jesus' eyes—as he sees you— who would you see?

{ *Don't give up on your dreams. Keep sleeping.* }

Describe how Jesus sees you here:

HOW MIGHT YOUR WORLD

[CHANGE]

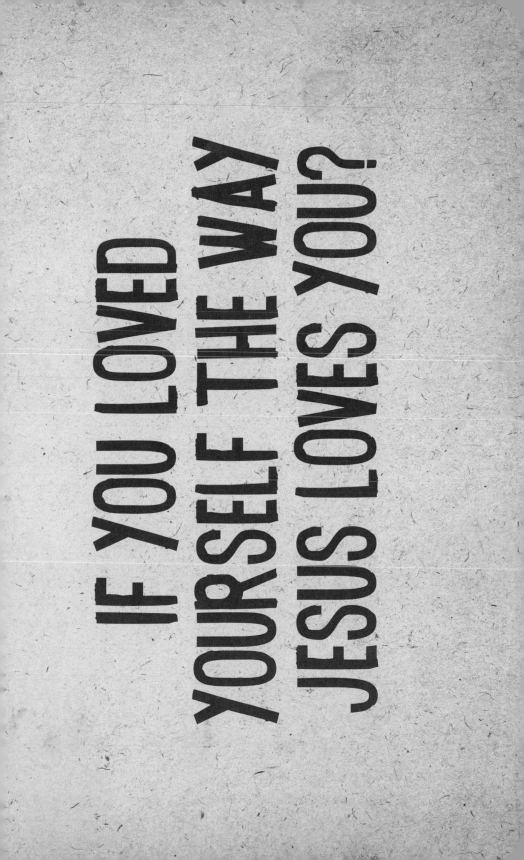

19

"Just do your job, Jesus."

When Jesus appeared on Earth, it had been nearly 1,000 years since Israel was at its peak under Solomon. The crowds expected Jesus to bring back those good old days, and, man, were they disappointed when he didn't.

Jesus didn't care about that. He was too busy staying on mission and message.

But it raises a question: Are you feeling disappointed in Jesus? Is he falling short of your expectations? If so, how?

{ *Isn't it weird that we have one hand that knows how to do everything and another that just sits there like, "I don't know how to hold a pencil"?* }

Go on, be honest. If you've got something to say, say it here:

20

Life's not fair...

Life's not fair. Just ask Jesus.

Born poor amid a swirl of questions concerning his parentage. A refugee in Egypt while still a toddler. Hunted by a ruler so desperate to kill him that he slaughtered innocent babies, just on the off-chance Jesus might be among them. Steered into a life of manual labor. Often homeless...misunderstood by his family... mocked by his community.

And then there's that whole crucifixion thing.

But Jesus chose it all. He stepped in between you and the consequences of your sin. He took the bullet for you...well, for all of us. But you, too.

Was that fair? No. Was it love? Yes.

{ *Get the "whys" right. When you know why you're doing something, it helps you make great decisions.* }

Thank Jesus here:

I LOVE ALL WHO LOVE ME. THOSE WHO SEARCH WILL SURELY FIND ME.

Proverbs 8:17, NLT

21

"What's up with the attitude?"

"Blessed are you when people insult you, persecute you and falsely say all kinds of evil against you because of me" (Matthew 5:11).

Jesus said that when people attack you because of him it's a blessing. That it's actually a good thing.

What he doesn't do is explain—at least not to everyone's satisfaction—*why*.

Roasted by skeptics, dismissed in class, kicked around at work... those are good things? In what universe are they *good* things?

Jesus, if it's not too much trouble, would you explain? Where's the upside? Where's the blessing?

{ *Practice empathy. Give others the benefit of the doubt. Do your best to put yourself in their shoes.* }

Talk to Jesus about any unwelcome
"blessings" you're dealing with here:

Random happy time. Doodle here. Daydream.

Feed your happiness

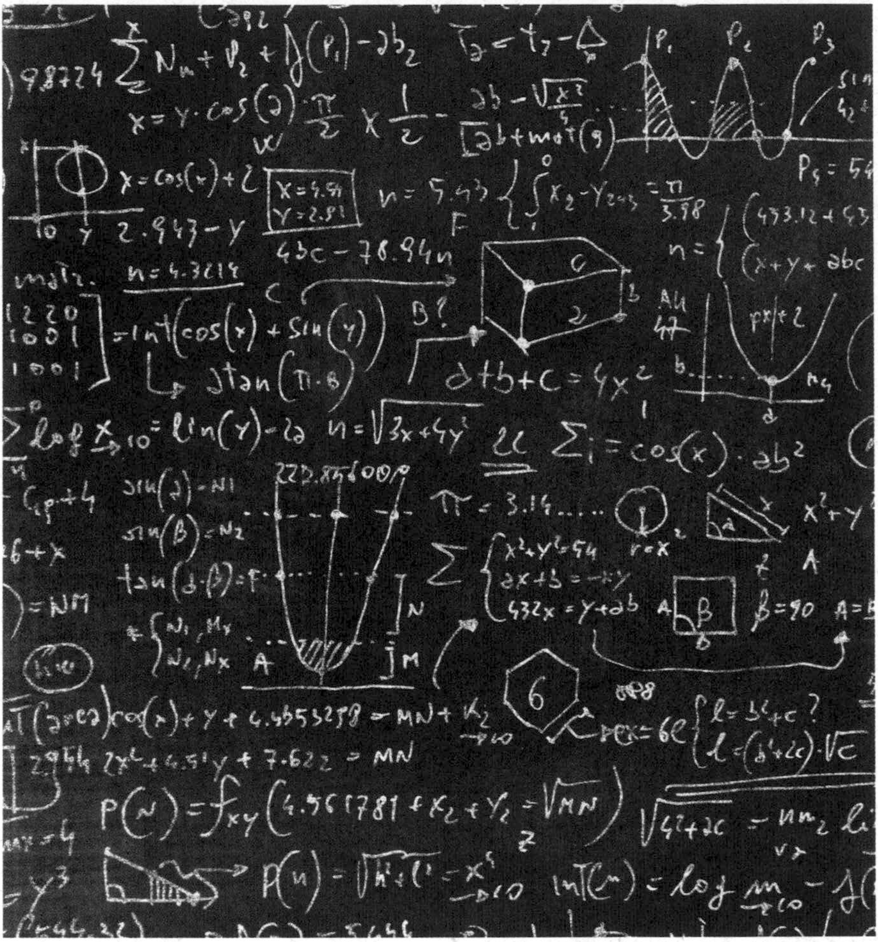

22

"Uh-oh..."

The world can be a scary place. Some days come with fangs.

The Bible says this: "There is no fear in love. But perfect love drives out fear" (1 John 4:18).

If you've invited Jesus—and his perfect love—into your world, why does fear still sometimes sink its claws into you? What's up with that?

Jesus encountered scary things, but he did so fearlessly, fueled by complete trust in his Father.

Consider what's fueling your fear in those moments your gut clenches. Is it a lack of confidence in yourself? in Jesus? Or is it something else? And what is "perfect love," and why does it sometimes seem unable to muscle fear out of our lives?

When you go out to eat, use that student ID. Get 10 percent off at Arby's, Buffalo Wild Wings, Dunkin' Donuts, Qdoba, and Subway. Even if it only gets you a free drink, hey, it's free.

Where are you experiencing fear in your life lately? Peel it back with Jesus' help. What might be prompting it?

AND MY GOD WILL MEET ALL YOUR NEEDS ACCORDING TO HIS GLORIOUS RICHES IN CHRIST JESUS.

Philippians 4:19

GUEST CHECK

DATE	SERVER	TABLE	QUESTS	CHECK NUMBER
				689561
			TAX	
			TOTAL	

Thank You - Please Come Again

23

"What happened to my paycheck?"

If you're hoping to get rich, don't steal a page from Jesus's playbook.

He didn't charge for public appearances, healing lepers, or raising the dead. And when he turned water into wine, he gave it away—for *free*. It's like the guy was allergic to making a buck.

Yet Jesus talked a *lot* about money—including being careful of always wanting more of what it can buy.

Jesus: a guy who could have charged astronomical fees for his services—but didn't go there. When you reflect on Jesus' generosity, his living with money but not being controlled by it, how does that color your view of him?

"Watch out! Be on your guard against all kinds of greed; life does not consist in an abundance of possessions" (Luke 12:15).

{ *Student poor: when you have too much month at the end of your money.* }

What is it you're really wanting when you want more money—and why?

What I want...

Why?

AS A STUDENT, THE MOST COMFORTING WORDS YOU'LL EVER HEAR ARE "I HAVEN'T STARTED EITHER."

24

"I will never, ever forgive her for that…"

Consider rethinking that position. Given, you know, what Jesus said:

"For if you forgive other people when they sin against you, your heavenly Father will also forgive you. But if you do not forgive others their sins, your Father will not forgive your sins" (Matthew 6:14-15).

Jesus! Did you *mean* that? What happened to all that unconditional love stuff I keep hearing about?

Jesus takes forgiveness seriously. If you follow him, you don't get the option of counting on his forgiveness while you reserve the right to hang on to bitterness toward someone else. Not going to happen.

So think of a hurt you're nursing, a grudge you're hauling around. Ask Jesus: How can I move past my pain to get to forgiveness? Where is an onramp to healing?

{ Communal showers exist. Say goodbye to privacy until Thanksgiving break. }

Ask Jesus to show you your own heart when it comes to forgiveness.

Color this space in a way.

that reflects what you've discovered.

25

"Woo-hoo!"

Now that you've graduated, you can do what you want, when you want—assuming you still show up on time. And get stuff done. And keep the Important People happy.

Still...freedom!

But what are you now free *from*...and free *for*? How you answer that question shapes pretty much everything moving forward.

Because, if you're a Jesus follower, you're already free. Free from...and free for. Jesus was clear from the beginning about why he'd come: "I have come to set captives free."

How is Jesus setting you free? In what ways are you no longer a captive? And what might Jesus have freed you to be...to do...to become?

{ *You have not experienced true fear until one of your posters falls down in the middle of the night.* }

"It is for freedom that Christ has set us free. Stand firm, then, and do not let yourselves be burdened again by a yoke of slavery."

Galatians 5:1

What did Jesus set you free from—and for?

BE FREE AND PREPARED.

Keep in your car and/or apartment

{ } rain poncho

{ } work gloves

{ } flashlight or headlamp (with extra batteries)

{ } simple first-aid kit

{ } reflective tape

{ } jumper cables

{ } foam tire sealant

{ } duct tape

{ } tow rope

{ } one bag kitty litter

{ } nonperishable protein bars

{ } filled water bottle

{ } foldable shovel

{ } warm blanket

{ } candle and waterproof matches

{ } some basic tools like hammer, screwdriver...

{ } packaging tape

{ } hand sanitizer

{ } camping knife

[ ] Ziploc bags

[ ] varied size bungee cords

[ ] 2' x 3' carpet sample

[ ] 2-3 glow sticks

[ ] printed list of important phone numbers

[ ] extra phone charge cable

[ ] eight-hour hand warmer

other:

_____

_____

_____

_____

_____

Great gift from a parent or relative:

One-year membership to AAA. The insurance, roadside assistance
(even for bike riders), restaurant discounts, store discounts, and
travel discounts make it a great investment for anyone just
starting out.

26

"What is *wrong* with this guy?"

Jesus' family thought he was crazy. Especially once Jesus squared off with big-time religious leaders who could—and would—hurt him.

People around Jesus hoped if he toned down the rhetoric the religious attack dogs might not bite.

But Jesus didn't much care. He stayed on message and mission. He'd already counted the cost and was willing to pay the price.

Some people are like that: sold out to a cause. They aren't about to back down, no matter what. Some we applaud as heroes. Others we pity as fools.

Which camp would you put Jesus in—and why? Was he a hero...a fool...or a hero that many people thought a fool?

(Check out Mark 3:31-33 for an awkward family encounter, Jesus-style.)

{ *How college students and babies are alike: Poor personal grooming, affinity for annoying music, erratic eating habits, pass out during lectures, would rather play than learn, clothes provided by parents, and likely to protest publicly.* }

Jesus, here's how I view you...and why:

why?

27

"I need some friends..."

Turns out your mom was right: You become like your friends. We all do. That's why choices about people are a game-changer.

Jesus hung out with notably bad influences: prostitutes, tax cheats, religious snobs. (Apparently his mom didn't love him enough to give him good advice.)

But Jesus came out okay—he never lost sight of who he was, never compromised what he believed just to fit in. He lived with integrity. And he lived to please his Father, not to meet the expectations and standards of the people around him.

{ *Friends are people who know you really well and like you anyway.—Greg Tamblyn* }

How do you think he pulled that off?
And how might you do the same thing?

_____

_____

_____

my plan

_____

_____

TIPS FOR MAKING FRIENDS THE FIRST FEW WEEKS AT COLLEGE

PUT YOURSELF IN PLACES WHERE POTENTIAL FRIENDS ARE. MEET, TALK, AND TRY TO FIND SOMETHING IN COMMON.

A HANDFUL OF PEOPLE KNOW HALF THE CAMPUS BY THE END OF THE THIRD DAY. DON'T WORRY ABOUT THEM. THEY REALLY ARE THE MINORITY.

IT'S OKAY TO INVITE YOURSELF TO TAG ALONG WITH SOME OF THE PROTO-GROUPS JUST STARTING. THEY'RE NEW AND NOT FORMED YET.

YOUR SOCIAL LIFE ISN'T DOOMED IF YOU HAVEN'T MADE SOME FRIENDS THE FIRST FEW WEEKS. IT CAN TAKE A COUPLE OF MONTHS OF TRYING NEW THINGS TO MEET NEW PEOPLE.

FRIENDS COME AND GO LIKE THE WAVES OF THE OCEAN...BUT THE TRUE ONES STAY LIKE AN OCTOPUS ON YOUR FACE.

28

"I'm too broke to give."

Okay, valid point: If you're piling up student debt, you probably don't have much of a charitable giving budget.

At least, in cash.

But what *can* you give? Giving frees up your spirit, shifts your focus off yourself, fuels gratitude, boomerangs huge satisfaction straight back at you.

Where can you volunteer time? mentor an at-risk child? come alongside someone who needs a listening ear? share lunch?

People are almost never too broke to give...just too broken.

That's why Jesus praised the widow who carefully placed her "mite" into the Temple collection pot, even when nobody else noticed her. Giving is about offering what you have, not about how your gift compares with what others give.

You're not too broke to give what you have to give, and Jesus makes beautiful, bountiful things out of next to nothing.

The Best Way to teach your kids about taxes is by eating 30 percent of their ice cream.
—Bill Murray

So make a quick list of how you
might be able to give back here:

A list is only a list unless you try something. Put a date
next to one of your items, and then do it.

LEARN TO DO GOOD

SEEK JUSTICE.
HELP THE OPRESSED;
DEFEND THE
ORPHAN; PLEAD FOR
THE WIDOW.

ISAIAH 1:17

DONE IN

29

"So much for managing my brand."

Admit it: You love recognition. No shame in that; most people appreciate a thumbs-up now and then.

But Jesus flipped that desire on its head when he said, "Your Father, who sees what is done in secret, will reward you" (Matthew 6:18).

Jesus is especially impressed with the good you do when nobody's looking. When nobody applauds and you don't post a selfie online.

But why? Why is Jesus so concerned about doing good offline? What do you think he's after? What does that say about him...and what he wants for you?

{ *Growing old is mandatory, but growing up is optional.* }
—Walt Disney

No, seriously. What do you think about all that?
Jot your thoughts here:

....

....

....

....

....

....

If there are some not so good things you're doing
when no one is looking and you want to change
that—what's your game plan?

Doodling
fun fact.

["Recent research in neuroscience, psychology and design shows that doodling can help people stay focused, grasp new concepts and retain information. A blank page also can serve as an extended playing field for the brain, allowing people to revise and improve on creative thoughts and ideas." —*Sue Shellenbarger*]

Go outside and bring this journal with you. Then doodle AND get some fresh air.

30

"How about you wait in the car?"

Road Trip Rule #17: With the right person, any trip's an adventure.

Want an adventure? Go with Jesus. He'll lead you to places you'd never think to visit on your own. Toss you in among the poor, the needy, the sinking, the interesting.

What if he steered you to the LBGTQ rally and you listened to hearts, not rhetoric? told you to strike up a conversation with that protester outside the abortion clinic? nudged you to stop by that frat party to be a designated driver?

Jesus went lots of places where he risked his reputation—but connected with people who needed him.

If you're apprehensive about where he might take you, maybe you don't yet understand the goodness of his heart. That the adventure he invites you into is less important than your traveling companion.

{ Awkward College Moment #5: Going to an event just for the free pizza then trying to think of an excuse to leave early. }

What might it look like to tag along with Jesus today?

It's the perfect day.

Today's the day. The day you throw back your arms and embrace the joy of Simply. Being. Alive.

Yeah, there's stuff you have to do, bills to pay, but, hey—hand them to Jesus to carry for you today. Let him haul them around awhile.

Consider: No matter what else is happening in your life, you're loved. You're a child of God. This is the day the Lord has made, and he's seen fit to drop you into it.

What's not to love about today? Why aren't you dancing? It's the perfect day to pause, take a deep breath, and remember why you're grateful for this life you've been given.

Awkward College Moment #7: Getting lost on campus the first week of college. Don't worry about forgetting everything from orientation; everybody does.

Create a "you are loved" playlist here that makes you want to dance. Then add it to your phone, hit play, and start dancing.

32

"I can't forget what I've done."

Regrets are punks. They beat you up, shifting your focus from the present to the past. They steal joy, suffocate peace. And they're always right there at the edge of the playground, smoking cigarettes, talking trash about you.

Let Jesus deal with them for you.

He'll help you forgive yourself. Go with you as you clean up any messes you made. And those punks? They're goners.

Jesus is in the giving-you-freedom-from-your-past business. But only if you ask him. And if you're willing to follow him away from those regrets and into a new life with him.

Roomate Note #4: Dear Jenny, you left me alone and undefended. Alas, I am no more. Love, The Cookies.

Draw some regrets with "x's" on their eyes here...

I am with you always, to the very end of the age.

—Jesus

Matthew 28:20

33

Who's along for the ride?

While planning a 1914 South Pole expedition, Ernest Shackleton worried—a lot—about who to take along.

With the right team he could weather the obstacles he'd encounter. But having the wrong people on board could be a disaster.

He was right. Shackleton's ship got stuck in pack ice, which chewed it up and eventually sank it. Thousands of miles from help, with no way to send an SOS, the men on that team worked together to find their way to safety.

That's how it works in life—including yours. Who's along for the ride helps...or hurts.

Who's with you on your journey? Are they helping—or hindering—where you need to be? Are they building you up or chipping away at you?

{ Got Cheetos crumbs in your keyboard? Just swipe the sticky part of a Post-it between the keys to get rid of them. }

1914 South Pole expedition team

**Ask Jesus: Which people in my life are
leading me closer to you—and why?**

Why?

Why?

Why?

34

Okay...worth a try.

Today talk with someone who makes you uncomfortable.

That homeless guy at the bus stop. The transgender working at the coffee shop. The fundamentalist Christian hauling around his 40-pound King James Bible. Anyone who doesn't look—or think—quite like you.

Say, "I've seen you around, but I don't know you." Then share your name and stick out your hand.

Jesus did stuff like that all the time, and it led to some fascinating encounters—conversations that were awkward, messy, and ultimately life-changing for so many.

Who have you seen lately who Jesus might be nudging you to talk with?

Never be afraid to try something new. Remember, amateurs built the ark; professionals built the Titanic.

What is it about people that makes you uncomfortable?
What are the barriers between you and others?

DO NOT BE AFRAID

THE PHRASE "DO NOT BE AFRAID" IS WRITTEN IN THE BIBLE 365 TIMES. THAT'S A DAILY REMINDER FROM GOD TO LIVE EVERY DAY WITHOUT FEAR.

35

"What? Are you *kidding* me?"

It's hard enough not to have sex. Now you can't even *think* about it?

Depends. There's thinking and there's *thinking*. Passing thoughts and focused "I wish I could" considerations.

That last one is what Jesus is talking about—and mostly because what we invite into our minds and hearts shapes us. Often not for the better.

Lust objectifies the people in our fantasies. poisons committed relationships. prompts guilt.

Suppose you and Jesus were talking about your sex life. (Yeah, creepy thought, but still...) What might he say?

"I tell you that anyone who looks at a woman lustfully has already committed adultery with her in his heart" (Matthew 5:28).

{ *"When you look at the dark side, careful you must be...for the dark side looks back."* }
  —Yoda

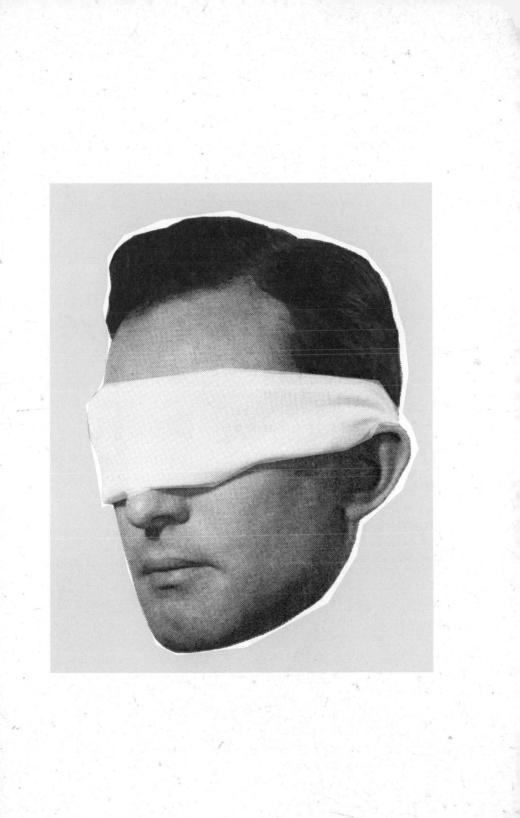

Okay, Jesus...let's talk sex...

Do not conform any longer to the pattern of this world, but be transformed by the renewing of your mind. Then you will be able to test and prove what God's will is—his good, pleasing, and perfect will.

Romans 12:2

36

"Oh, man, was that me?"

Yeah, it was. You did it. That was you.

Maybe nobody else noticed, but you can play it back frame by frame.

And you feel...shame.

Shame's toxic, gnawing at your soul, stinging like acid in your eyes. It points a smirk your way and says, "Yeah—that thing you did? That's you. That's who you are."

But that's *not* who you are. It's *not* the sum total of a person Jesus died to redeem. You're more than what you've done—even if you left chalk outlines on the floor.

You are, simply, who Jesus says you are. Nothing more, nothing less. And that's good news because he calls you his beloved.

You are a *child of God*. A child who may need to ask forgiveness, who's got some consequences to shoulder, but you are *not* what you've done.

{ *My favorite childhood memory is not paying bills.* }

That lie will suck the life out of you. Without getting too specific (who knows who'll read this), jot down some of the lies you've come to believe about yourself.

HOW TO BE ASSERTIVE WITHOUT BEING...
YOU KNOW

[ ] Stay respectful as you state your case directly and openly.

[ ] Use "I" statements—own your feelings and decisions.

[ ] Be confident.

[ ] Don't feel you need to explain or justify your feelings or opinions.

[ ] Pick your battles. What's important to you, and what can you let slide?

LANDING THAT JOB AFTER HIGH SCHOOL

- [ ] Brushing your tongue helps get rid of bad breath.
- [ ] Dress appropriately. Find pictures of employees to use as a guide.
- [ ] Be prepared. Have copies of your résumé. Take notes.
- [ ] Practice answering both behavioral and competency questions.
- [ ] Recipe for relaxation: Exhale completely, inhale four seconds, hold your breath seven seconds, and exhale eight seconds.
- [ ] Be on time.
- [ ] Everyone matters. The receptionist is as key as a department leader.
- [ ] Firm handshake and eye contact are helpful.
- [ ] Calm yourself and let the real you come out.
- [ ] Be sure you can answer the question "Why do you want to work here?"
- [ ] Afer a job interview, if asked, "Do you have any questions?" always say, "Yes. Is there anything about my application that concerns you?"

37

"I can't take any more!"

Life can be challenging. Especially right about now.

New problems fly at you nonstop. Stuff to pay for. Things to do. People to please.

Growing up isn't always fun.

But Jesus is with you and—if you're willing—will use those challenges to shape you. To feed your humility. Inspire endurance. Shape your character.

Which should come as no surprise, actually. He's an artist, working in the medium of...you.

To give you hope...in him.

So lean into Jesus. Ask him to make the most of this time to transform you into the person he's created you to be.

Remember that guy who gave up? Neither does anyone else.
—Unknown

Ask Jesus: What can I learn about myself—and you—as I walk through this?
Jot what you hear below:

....

....

....

....

....

....

38

"Ack! I'm overwhelmed!"

Welcome to your world: New job. New classes. New place to live. New schedule.

Take a deep breath. You've survived other transitions, and you'll survive this one.

God *designed* you for transitions—for transformation.

The Apostle Paul wrote this: "Anyone who belongs to Christ has become a new person. The old life is gone; a new life has begun!" (2 Corinthians 5:17, NLT).

{ *It's okay to not be okay all the time.* }

So don't panic. Instead, ask Jesus what he has in mind as you round the bend into this next season of your life. Really—ask him. Jot what you hear.

_____

_____

_____

_____

_____

_____

_____

I can do everything through Christ who gives me strength.

PHILIPPIANS 4:13

Daisy
She loves me...
She loves me not.
She loves me...
She loves me not.

I don't know if she loves me,
And not knowing makes me nuts,
But one thing is for certain:
This daisy hates my guts.
—D.G. Mason

English major's essay response: This poem, addressing uncertainty in romance, encapsulates an early mid-century ambiguity concerning blurring gender roles and relational power. Or it could be about an abused flower. Whichever explanation gets me the higher grade.

39

"How do I decide?"

Maybe you've heard about it: The Plan.

That perfect one God has for your life and, if you follow it, you're golden.

Except God hasn't pulled back the curtain to reveal which major to pick. job to take. person to date.

Is that because there *is* no plan...or because God doesn't like you enough to spell it out for you? Or maybe it's something else.

Maybe—just maybe—it's less about a perfect "plan" and more about the perfect heart of Jesus. Maybe the deepest calling is to know his heart, not his plans.

But with so many decisions needing to be made, you've got to do something, so do this: Talk with Jesus about them. See what he's got to say.

P.S. That may have been The Plan all along.

P.P.S. Now walk away from the daisy before one of you gets hurt.

{ *Don't put in the window what ain't in the warehouse.* }

**Jesus, it'd be great if you'd weigh
in about these issues in my life:**

40

But did he really mean it?

Here's what Jesus said about himself: "I am the **way** and the **truth** and the **life**. No one comes to the Father except through me" (John 14:16).

Three words. That's all it took to yank "truth" away from the philosophers and wrap it in skin.

Jesus said it's him. He's the Truth. Truth isn't a concept; it's not abstract; it's him. The person of Jesus. When we know him, we know Truth. He's not pointing *at* the truth, or talking *about* the truth, or arguing about what's true and what isn't—he's *embodying* the truth. Truth is standing there looking at you.

But that quote's a deal breaker for some people.

How could Jesus be so exclusive? so narrow? What about other holy men and women? Other messages about how to approach God?

But there it is. It's what he said. It is what it is.

What you do with it is up to you.

{ *Life isn't measured by the number of breaths you take, but by the number of moments that take your breath away.* }

You know the Truth...personally.
What's the Truth saying to you today?

If you've answered the truth question, tear these pages out and place them where they can be a constant visual reminder to you. Now be free.

And you will know the truth,

and the truth will set you free.

John 8:32

Free-range

doodling

![Photograph of a note reading "Pay ridiculous attention to Jesus" attached to a bicycle wheel]

Any time can be Jesus-centered time

Just a quick ride across campus to your next class...Or a chance to slow down and pay attention to Jesus? When we invite Jesus to interrupt every moment in our lives—not just the quiet, calm ones—suddenly even daily classes take on a whole new purpose.

For resources that help you pay ridiculous attention to Jesus, visit **MyLifetree.com**

Where will Jesus interrupt you?

#Jesusinterruption